EUGENIO PUCCI

S0-AKF-227

ALL ROME
AND THE VATICAN

Translated by
NANCY WOLFERS MAZZONI

BONECHI EDITORE

50122 FLORENCE - 5, Via dei Rustici

Rappresentante concessionario per Roma e Lazio:

Ditta **MA. PI. R.** di Mario Pietrangeli
Via delle Fornaci, 153-155
00165 ROMA
Tel. **6.375.259**

Direttore Responsabile **VITTORIO CUMINETTI**
Condirettore **GIAMPAOLO BONECHI**

Stampa: Arti Grafiche Parigi & Maggiorelli - Firenze
Fotolito - LA FOTOLITOGRAFIA - Firenze
Servizio Fotografico eseguito da GAETANO BARONE

Autorizzazione del Tribunale di Firenze n. 1835 del 31-5-67
Spedizione a tariffa editoriale ridotta

© Copyright 1968 by BONECHI EDITORE - FIRENZE
Via dei Rustici, 5 - Telefono 298.224-25

Printed in Italy - Proprietà letteraria riservata
Riproduzione anche parziale vietata

Finito di stampare in Firenze nel Settembre 1972

HISTORICAL INTRODUCTION

We shall not repeat here the now well-known legend of the founding of Rome, that speaks of Aeneas, Romulus, Remus, and the famous seven kings. However, it is from the legend of Romulus and Remus (the sons of Rea Silva and the God Mars, abandoned on the waters of the Tiber, and suckled by a she-wolf) that Rome derives its symbol. In fact, today in the Capitoline Museum of the Palace of the Conservatori we find the she-wolf, an Etruscan work of the first half of the fifth century B.C. Originally the sculpture did not have the two charming « putti » in the act of suckling milk. These were added in 1400 by the great Florentine sculptor Antonio del Pollaiolo.

There are various theories regarding the derivation of the name « Rome ». Some scholars maintain that it comes from the word « Rumon ». At the period of its founding, which according to Varrone took place on April 21, 753 B.C., this was the name given to the River Tiber. Other scholars tend to identify Rome with the word « ruma » (breast), the name given to the Palatine Hill which has a geological formation recalling the form of a breast. However far into the legendary past its roots may lie, there was a beginning for the Eternal City. This beginning dates from the pre-historic period when a Latin population established itself on the hills of the Tiber valley. This population came under the strong influence of the Etruscans who in the seventh century B.C. dominated Lazio and Campania. The Latins and the Etruscans did have many things in common: religion, commercial regulations, law code, military procedures, and the same symbol of executive power, a bundle of rods. Soon the Latins dominated over the Etruscans and as sovereigns divided the people into two social categories, the aristocracy and the plebeians. The power was in the hands of the aristocracy, but the plebeians, under the leadrship of their « tribunes » attained civil and political equality. These changes took place during the fourth and fifth century B.C.

As soon as the Roman Republic achieved a certain social and political equilibrium, they began to survey the regions surrounding them. They understood that it they wanted to maintain commercial supremacy and guarantee security, it was necessary to extend their power over Lazio. Therefore, in the fifth century B.C., they defeated the Sabines, the Aequi, and the Volsci in a war which allowed them to form the Latin League. In the fourth century B.C., the Romans conquered the Veii, but they were defeated in a conflict with the Senone Gauls who left Rome in ruins. When they had recovered from these conflicts, and were once more masters of Lazio, there were more arduous battles with the Samnites. But they also triumphed over these people, and were able to establish a strong state in Central Italy. The desire for conquest had been awakened, however, and now, Rome looked to the Greek colonies in the southern part of the peninsula, where internal dissension played into the hands of the enemy. Their ever increasing power cast a shadow over Taranto which declared war on them with the help of Pyrrus, King of Epirus. The latter attained many military successes, until he was called to help his allies Siracusa and Agrigento who were defending themselves against attacks on the sea by the powerful Carthaginians. When he returned to Italy, he found the Roman army barring his way at Benevento. Defeated, he was obliged to return to his own country. This incident brought an end to the Greek colonies in Italy. One by one they were conquered by the Romans, whose domain now extended from the Macron and the Rubicon to the Straits of Messina.

It now became necessary for the Romans to come to terms with the powerful Carthaginians who dominated the Mediterranean controlling Sicily, Sardinia and Corsica. They were a real threat to Roman security. A bitter battle took place, but the Romans emerged as victors despite the valour of the Carthaginians and the military prowess of their leaders Hannibal and Hasdrubal. While the Roman armies were fighting against the Eastern people who had helped the Carthaginians, this great rival was conquered by Scipio Africanus in the famous Battle of Zama. The territory of Carthage became a Roman province when Carthage fell in the year 146 B.C. During the wars against Carthage, and afterwards, Rome conquered Cisalpine Gaul, occupied the whole of Northern Italy, Istria, Macedonia and Greece. But as Roman power grew, their economic and industrial possibilities also grew. Consequently, a few people became wealthy who used their capital to their own advantage and provoked economic crises, « servile wars », and a revolt of the proletariat. In 133 B.C., Tiberius Sempronius Gracdus, supporting the cause of the plebeians, tried to introduce some lawful reforms but the rich landowners opposed and had him killed. In 123, however, his brother Gaius was elected Tribune of the people and succeeded with certain reforms. A man of broad vision, he extended the right of Roman citizenship to Latins and to the other populations of the peninsula. In this way he consolidated the unity of the peninsula. But the Roman people did not want to share their sovereignty. The Tribune was not re-elected, and after various incidents was driven to suicide. Jugartha of Numidia, who had ambitions of power, became an enemy of Rome. An army, commanded by the Consul Quintus Caecilius Metellus was sent to subdue him but did not succeed. In 107 B.C., Gaius Marius, who had been elected Consul, took his place. Jugartha was defeated, and the Cimbrians and the Teutons who had invaded Italy in that period were conquered in two famous battles. Marius became the most powerful man of Rome. During Marius's absence from Rome, dissatisfaction regarding the agrarian laws was intensified. With the Tribune Saturninius, the former attempts for reform of the Gracchi were renewed. But the aristocracy was opposed to any change. Marius was compelled to quell their resistance with force, and during this turbulent period, Saturninius was killed. The agitation for reform continued, and even increased under the Tribune Livius Drusus in 91 B.C. Like Gaius Graccus, it was his program to extend Roman citizenship to the Italic populations. But Drusus was killed as well. In 90 B.C. his death provoked an Italic league composed of Sabellian and Oscan people to combat against Roman tyranny. They were successful and even won the support of the Umbrians and Etruscans. At this point the Senate realized its error and at the proposal of Lucius Julius Caesar, granted the right of citizenship. But part of the league did not accept the terms of the treaty: Nola, Samnium, Lucania, and Bruttium resisted in the hope that King Mithridates of Pontus would come to their aid. However, in 97 B.C. the Roman Consul Lucius Cornelius Silla was sent to fight against this ruler, conquered him and returned to Italy. In the meantime, in Rome Marius who had profited by his rival's absence, had died. In order to reenter the Eternal City, Silla had to face a democratic army commanded by Marius's son. The latter were defeated and the power of the Senate prevailed. But in 79 B.C. Silla died and power reverted to the democratic leadership of Gneius Pompey and Marcus Licinius Crassus.

These two men were faced with a critical situation in both domestic and foreign affairs. A revolt of the slaves had to be suppressed;

Mithridates had declared war against Rome again; and pirates had invaded the seas of the Empire imperiling navigation and the lines of communication. Pompey had become very powerful, but now another leader by the name of Gaius Julius Caesar was gaining ascendency. Together with Crassus, Caesar championed the cause of a more equitable distribution of land, which would alleviate the poverty of the plebeians, and form a larger class of small landowners. This proposal was opposed by Cicero. An ambitious man named Lucius Sergius Catilina, who stirred the common people by promising the dissolving of debts and the confiscation of the property of the rich, gained a considerable following. But this revolutionary was defeated by the eloquence of Cicero, his armies were dispersed, and he was killed near Pistoia. Pompey re-established order in Rome and formed a triumvirate with Caesar and Crassus. Caesar, elected Consul, put the agrarian laws into use, and was assigned the government of the Gallic provinces where the people were conspiring against Rome. The Helvetians, the Gauls, and the Teutons attempted military uprisings, but were combatted by the military genius of Caesar. Meanwhile, in Rome, Pompey had become a real dictator backed by the Senate. Crassus had died and Caesar, upon returning from Gaul, was ordered to disband his army. He refused, and marched on Rome forcing Pompey and his army to withdraw to Greece. Becoming dictator, Caesar first had to defeat his rivals in Spain and then Pompey himself in Greece, in the famous Battle of Pharsalus which took place on August 9, 48 B.C.

From this moment on, the Roman Republic no longer existed. Caesar was not only a military genius but also a great statesman. He subjected the entire East, reconciled Asia and Greece, defeated the rest of his enemies at Thapsus and in Spain, and initiated useful reforms in every field. On March 15, 44 B.C. a conspiracy plotted against him and he was murdered. The purpose of the conspiracy was to re-establish « Republican liberty », but they did not succeed. Power was assumed by Mark Anthony and Gaius Julius Octavian, nephew of Caesar. They fought the forces of the two principal conspirators Brutus and Cassius at the Battle of Philippi in Macedonia. Mark Anthony parted for the East to meet the Parthians in battle. In Egypt, he succumbed to the beautiful Cleopatra, and joined his forces against Rome. Octavian, in Rome, using statesman-like strategy and the force of arms, had to confront the opposition at home. He succeeded and became the absolute leader in the West. He defeated Anthony in the Battle of Actium in Greece and provoked the suicide of Anthony and Cleopatra. Octavian returned to Rome where the Senate awarded him the title of « Imperator », Farther of the Country. They proclaimed him « Augustus », that is, divine, the title with which he is remembered in history. During his leadership, from the year 8 B.C. to 9 A.D., the entire Empire was at peace. In one of the more restless of the Roman provinces, Palestine, Jesus of Nazareth was born.

The Imperial Age followed with the reign of the Claudians, the Flavians, and the Antonines. The enormous Roman Empire was governed more or less wisely and the emperors were often obliged to send their legions to quiet rebellions. The Roman people were subjected to an absolute authority that was based on military force and the will of various despots. Many of these, however, were wise and courageous rulers assisted by personalities who have become famous in history for their versatility and intellectual gifts. It is during this period, from Tiberius to the Emperor Constantine, that the great mystical force of Christianity spread throughout the Empire. In the year 41, the Apostles Peter and Paul began to preach and their work was continued by their successors through the centuries. This new spiritual force of Christianity became dominant at a period when the Roman Empire of the West was decaying. The Christian Church took up the political, judiciary, cultural, and artistic legacy of Rome, and preserved it throughout the period of the barbaric invasions. By means of the principles of Christian doctrine, the people who had been subjugated by Roman force and genius, learned to value its greatness and beneficence. The division of the hugh Roman Empire occurred after the death of Theodosius the Great (395 A.D.), under whose reign Christianity had become the state religion. The Eastern Empire had another thousand years of life, while the Western Empire ceased to exist in less than a century. The division of the Roman Empire brought great consequences in every field. In the West, the barbaric invasions took place. On August 24, 410, Alaric sacked Rome. In 452, Attila attempted the same thing and razed Aquileia to the ground. But when he arrived on the banks of the Mincio he changed his mind. Pope Leo I interceded to save Rome and Attila retraced his steps. The Eastern Empire had done its best to save the West from barbarians, but there were domestic troubles to contend with, and the task was too great. Odoacre, one of the chieftains of the Vandals and of the Franks who had already taken over Northern Italy, brought an end to the Western Empire in 476. He was now in control of the whole Italian peninsula.

During the period of the barbarian invasions, and during the Middle Ages, the history of Rome is actually the history of the Church of Rome, and of the popes, who were the leaders and defenders of the faith. At the beginning, Rome did not break her ties with the Eastern Empire where in 435-39, the great Justinian tried to rebuild the Western Empire. But after two centuries of these events, Rome became a truly pontifical state; as a result of the activity of Charlemagne it temporarily became the center of European politics with the establishment of the Holy Roman Empire. Shortly thereafter, in 1144, the Municipal Age began in Rome, when the papacy, the commune, the nobility, and the rather remote power of the emperor struggled for supremacy. It was a turbulent period in which the Seat of the Papacy was transferred to Avignon (1305-1377). This permitted the establishment of a popular government for a certain period. But with the return of the Popes to Rome, the power of this government was reduced. From this moment on, the temporal power of the popes became increasingly stronger. Once again, the papacy was to make Rome not only the center of Christianity, but also a real cultural and artistic capital of the world.

The actions of the popes were not always beyond reproach. There were struggles for political power, wars, religious schisms and elections of popes and antipopes. But there were also popes of mighty stature, such as Martin V; Eugenius IV who presided over the Florentine Council of 1439 to reunite the Latin and the Orthodox church; the great humanistic Pope Nicholas V, during whose reign the Christian Empire at Constantinople fell to the Turks; Callisto III, who organized a crucade against the Turks; the learned Pius II Piccolomini, founder of the Universities of Basilea, of Nantes, and of Ingolstadt; the great reformer Paul II; Sixtus IV, the astute politician who dedicated his energies to defending Christianity from Moslem intrusions; Innocent VIII, generous patron of art and letters; the highly intelligent Alexander VI, whose life was certainly not exemplary, but who was an able administrator, the organizer of missions for the diffusion of Christianity, and a patron of the arts; Julius II della Rovere, the great warrior pope, founder of Italian independence, and patron of famous artists; Leo X of the Medici family, patron of artists and writers, and intelligent politician who was, however, unable to stem the Reformation or understand its causes; Clement VII of the Medici, during whose pontificate the terrible sack of Rome (1527) took place. After this tragic event, Rome recovered her strength and continued under the protection of the Catholic Church, assuming a great importance for Christianity in the period of the Counter-Reformation. This period (1543-1565) was from the pontificate of Paul III to Pius IV. With the Council of Trent (1545), which lasted eighteen years, the Catholic Church issued its « Magna Charta » in opposition to the Protestant Reformation. Five popes participated in this Council.

After this momentous event, other notable popes assumed the leadership of the Catholic Church: St. Pius V, Dominican, Pope of the Battle of Lepanto; Gregory VIII, remembered in history for his reform of the calendar; the stern Sixtus V to whom we owe a large part of the building development in Rome; the Florentine Urban VIII who reformed the clergy, the seminaries, the breviaries, encouraged missions, and patronized the arts. There were other popes of distinction in the field of religion, if not in politics. During the seventeenth and eighteenth centuries, the

Holy See followed a policy, more or less neutral, but during the tempestuous time of the French Revolution, the temporal powers of the Church were threatened. French armies invaded Italy, and proclaimed the Republic in Rome. They deported Pope Pius VI to France where he died on August 29, 1799. Pius VII, Barnabas Chiaramonti di Cesena was his successor. Meanwhile, Napoleon's attitude toward the papacy had changed, since he realized the pope might prove useful in furthering his dynastic aspirations, both at home, and in the field of international politics.

During the period of relative tranquillity that followed the downfall of Napoleon, the vision of a united and independent Italy began to kindle the imagination of the Italians. The election of Pope Pius IX, in 1846, greatly pleased Italian patriots, because they thought that the newly elected pope had liberal sentiments. One of his first acts was to declare amnesty for political prisoners, freedom of the press, and the right of the people to hold meetings. These acts provoked an enthusiasm which was exaggerated considering the political reality of the moment. Pope Pius IX was strong in religious zeal, but politically he was inept. He accepted the Ministry of Count Terenzio Mamiani, but the Minister was forced to resign, because of military and political pressure. The reaction favored a government under Pellegrino Rossi but he was stabbed by the revolutionaries who besieged the Pope at the Quirinal Palace demanding a constitution and a proclamation of the Republic. The ambassadors of France and Bavaria helped Pope Pius IX to escape on the evening of November 24, 1848. He fled from Rome to Gaeta where he took refuge with the King of Naples.

In Rome, as soon as the patriots heard the news, did not lose any time. On February 9, 1849 they proclaimed the Constitution of the Roman Republic and divested the Pope of all temporal power. A triumvirate was formed with Giuseppe Mazzini, Aurelio Saffi and Carlo Armellini, while Garibaldi, with a group of volunteers from Lombardy assumed the task of defending the new Republic. But the Republic did not last for long. The French landed eight thousand men at Civitavecchia forcing the surrender of the heroic defenders of the Roman Republic. The Pope returned on April 12, 1850. But the hope for Italian independence was not entirely lost. After ten years of ceaseless diplomatic and military negotiations, the great political genius, Cavour succeeded in having the Kingdom of Italy proclaimed on March 17, 1861. However it was a Kingdom without a true capital. After the death of Cavour, the Italian go-

vernment transferred the capital of the new Kingdom from Turin to Florence. Taking advantage of the war which had broken out between France and Prussia, and assuring the various nations that the Pope would not be endangered, the government ordered General Raffaele Cadorna to enter the Pontifical State with fifty thousand men. On September 19, 1870 Rome was beseiged; on the next day, the artillery succeeded in establishing a breach at Porta Pia, and the « bersaglieri » entered the city. On July 1, 1871 Rome finally became the capital of a united Italy.

The Pope, retiring within the gates of the Vatican Palace, considered himself a prisoner. He had refused to accept the terms of the treaty offered by the Italian government to regulate the relations between Church and State. His successors followed the same policy. Finally, on February 11, 1929 Pope Pius XI and the Italian government brought an end to the famous « Roman Question » by establishing the « Concordat », a peace treaty satisfactory to both parties. Since that time, the papacy, free of secular worries, has accomplished its evangelical mission with great zeal and has endeavored to establish peace among all the nations of the world. Pope Pius XII, who did his best to ward off the Second World War, left the Vatican to visit the Italian Royal family to try and convince them to stay out of the war, but it was useless. It was through his efforts, however, that Rome emerged from the war almost intact, except for some sporadic Anglo-American bombardments, and the German occupation. The city was liberated on June 4, 1944. Following a referendum on June 2, 1946 the Royal House of Savoy was deposed and Rome became the Capital of the Italian Republic.

We should note that Pius XII followed the example of his predecessors, when he left the Vatican to bless and encourage the Roman people after the bombings of the city. His predecessor, after the Lateran Pact, had left the Vatican for the first time to go to Castel Gandolfo. When Pius XII died at his summer residence of Castel Gandolfo on October 9, 1958, he was mourned by all of Rome. His successor, Pope John XXIII left the Vatican for a more extensive visit to Loreto and Assisi. Pope Paul VI, in the first week of January, 1964, went on a holy pilgrimage to the Holy Land, travelling by air. He was the first Pope after St. Peter, to visit Palestine and the sacred places where Jesus spent His life on earth.

A view of the **Roman Forum:** in the foreground the remains of the pronaos of the **Temple of Saturn.** On the right what is left of the **Basilica Giulia** with five naves, then the podium and three columns of the **Temple of Castor and Pollux.** Halfway down, the **Column of Foca,** on the left the **Temple of Antonino and Faustina** (actual church of San Lorenzo in Miranda), next to it, the **Temple of the Divus Romulus** and the Basilica of Constantine or of Maxentius and at the bottom, the **Church of Santa Francesca Romana** with a foreshortening of the Colosseum.

ANCIENT ROME

To admire and « to know how to look at » the ruins of ancient Rome means to listen to the breathing of the centuries which for the Eternal City — according to scholars — began nine hundred years before the coming of Christ. The breathing, not at all tiring, is lighter for the remote past, but acquires fullness and vitality slowly as we approach the present, which could never have existed if not for the illustrious past even if it is cloaked in legends. But the Roman people are extremely adherent to reality. They do not trust flights of fantasy. Even in their mythical legends man is always the principal protagonist whose intelligence and creative capacity in the social, moral and material order is the fulcrum around which the history of civilization turns.

This essential virtue of having everything serve as the measure of man in such a lasting way as to defy the centuries, is discovered by visitors to Rome today who see its traces as soon as they leave the Termini Station. They see it in the ruins of the grandiose wall which once encircled the city and which according to tradition was constructed by King Servio Tullio. The wall may be considered, in its defensive structure, the fundamental architectural element; that is the

first urbanistic sign of the future metropolis. It would be at the center of Roman expansion along the roads of the universe known at that time. From that moment on, the Roman people acquired a consciousness of themselves. They produced only that which was practically useful to the individual or to the group whether it dealt with the laws governing communal life in every field, or in their civil and military constructions.

The slow and continuous assertion of Roman power is always dominated by concrete facts. One has only to look at the bridges, granaries, cisterns, acqueducts, heated baths, gates, and markets. When the Italian peninsula was won over to the Roman cause, it became necessary for the Romans to maintain the respect of the various districts in Europe that had been conquered by their political and military genius. They built great communication roads layed out with very solid, smooth blocks impressive in length and width and demonstrating a fine technical know-how. These roads were a true testimony of an inflexible will that cut through hills and crossed over mountains. They scattered everywhere an indelible imprint of villages, towns, and cities not founded haphazardly but according to the su-

preme strategic and logistic interests of the grandiose metropolis which for centuries was considered the brain and the heart of the world. No other city on earth is capable of giving the visitor a more alive sense of the infinite, the universal, the majestic, and the famous. Observing the city under any aspect, we may see from the most distant past to the present, that she remains faithful to the primitive criterion of her founders and continuers; that is, to make the work of her talented statesmen, generals, architects, and builders durable in time.

Today we may admire the famous arches of ancient Rome, but few of us realize that before becoming famous, the Roman round arch was the unmistakable sign of Roman civilization. Whereever the Roman legions passed, architects introduced this type of arch in their bridges. It permitted them to provide for the requirements of war using at the same time solid singular aesthetic forms.

One may say that the architecture of the ancient city is dominated by the round arch: bridges, basilicas, famous arches, luxury residences, and public buildings bear this architectural element. Il will be adopted again in later constructions which, as the centuries go by, are added to the antique structures. At its height, Roman architecture satisfied its whims by employing a curvilinear concept in its buildings. This was opposed to the rectilinear concept used by the Greeks. The dome which is a spherical element was exploited in buildings with a circular plan. The round arch and its derivations led to the beautiful triumphal arches of Titus, Septimius Severus, Constantine, and Giano Quadrifronte. The dome element, together with Hellenistic influences, was employed in the construction of temples dedicated to the gods. Moreover, the Romans had a partiality for the rectangular form and internal colonades in the construction of basilicas. For theatres, amphitheatres, and circuses, they created ponderous conceptions adopting a curvilinear structure.

If the Romans were very sensible in adopting various architectural forms for their public and private buildings, they were not less so towards statuary art. In early times, when Rome was intent on becoming powerful and dominating other peoples, sculpture was left to Greek and Etruscan artists. Towards the second century before Christ, however, the rulers of public works began to be interested in the fine arts. They saw in sculpture a means of handing down to posterity the deeds of their captains and emperors, and the appearance of those who became famous in public life. This sculpture which dealt with historical reality was, in the period of the Roman Republic, characterized by a Greek style. But in the Augustan period sculptors rejected Hellenistic inspiration and chose the subjects for their works from living reality.

So, the historical relief and the portrait, the most important manifestations of Roman sculpture, came about to celebrate the deeds of the emperors. It is enough to remember the classic examples of the very famous « Ara Pacis Augustae » in Via di Ripetta, the interior reliefs of the Arch of Titus, Trajan's Column, and numerous other monuments. The artists knew how to obtain admirable pictorial effects in this particular type of ornamental sculpture. The Roman sculptors excelled also in the field of portraiture. Emperors and illustrious men were represented not only with their physical characteristics, but psychologically so that studying them we can only guess at their virtues and defects.

No less interesting for us is the Roman pictorial art. It is first found on the walls of luxurious dwellings of the metropolis, in Pompei and Herculanium. This art form dates from the second century before Christ to the second century after Christ. Archeologists have defined it stylistically as being Greco-Roman, since Greek masters were the first to adopt it in Italy. Examples may be seen in the decorations of the Villa Farnesina, the Casa di Livia on the Palatine, and the Casa di Esquilino. Not only were the Roman artists masters of mural painting but they were also experts in stucco and mosaic decoration.

A beautiful view of the **Way of the Imperial Forums.** In the foreground the **Forum of Caesar** in which the three beautiful Corinthian columns belonging to the Temple of the Mother Venus stand out. In the background is the impressive mass of the Colosseum.

THE ROMAN FORUM

The ideal reconstruction of the Roman Forum was made possible by archeologists who had studied the remains of grandiose buildings which, in every age have come to light in excavations. The first were undertaken at the beginning of the nineteenth century on French initiative and they have continued until out time. These archeologists tell us that the Roman Forum constituted the heart of the metropolis. Rich with temples, basilicas, monumental constructions of public function and beautiful statuary, one can understand why the Romans of the Republican and Imperial Age spoke of it with pride. In fact, in this Forum, the intensive political, civil, and religious life of the people took place.

Originally, the locality of the Forum was a swampy zone containing several water streams. The draining of the swamps was made possible by the construction of canals at the time of the primitive city. The place was destined to become a public market and took the name of Forum from the Latin « foras », a term which, in this case, means a

The column of the **Emperor Foca** in the center, on the left the **Arch of Septimius Severus,** and on the right the **Church of the Saints Martina and Luca** standing on the ruins of the *Secretarium Senatus*.

On the left in the foreground, a tract of the **Sacred Way;** at the center, the **Arch of Septimius Severus** behind which can be seen the back of the Altar of the Patria. To the left of the Altar is the *Tabularium*, the State Archives of ancient Rome, upon which the Palace of the Senate rises. The façade of this palace faces the Piazza del Campidoglio.

space outside the urban agglomeration. After the inhabitants of various hill towns united into a single community, this market came to be at the center of the established city of Rome. Little by little it lost its initial function, giving way to a grandiose complex of buildings destined for the political and administrative life of the Republic.

The Forum was devastated during various fires: the first at the beginning of the Republic; the second during the reign of Nero in 64 A.D.; the third under the Emperor Commodo; the fourth at the time of the Emperor Carino in 238. Disastrous earthquakes and barbaric invasions contributed to the distruction of the Forum. During the Middle Ages, the ruins were used as building material for houses and palaces. The area on which it once stood became pasture for cattle. Even the name was cancelled since it came to be called « Cow's Field ».

The **Sacred Way** flanked by antique temples. In the background the **Arch of Titus.**

A suggestive view of the **Roman Forum** taken from the Campidoglio. On the left, three beautiful Corinthian columns, the conspicuous remains of the **Temple of Vespasian.** On the right, the eight columns and architrave which constituted the pronaos of the **Temple of Saturn.** Immediately behind it is the **Arch of Septimius Severus,** and in the background the **Church of the Saints Martina and Luca.**

In the foreground the remains of the **Temple of Vesta,** on the left the little **Temple of Divus Romulus** son of Maxentius, in the background the **Church of Santa Francesca Romana.**

As has already been mentioned, at the beginning of the nineteenth century the first methodical archeological exploration of the Forum was begun on French initiative. It was continued by the Popes Pius VII, Gregory XVI, Pius IX, and, after the unity of Italy, by the Italian government which still provides for it. Worthy of merit during the time of the excavations of the Forum were Carlo Fea (1803-19), Cristiano Bunsen and L. Canina (1835-48), P. Rosa (1871-75), Giuseppe Fiorelli (1878-80), Rodolfo Lanciani (1882-86) and Giacomo Boni in 1898.

Two panoramic views of the **Roman Forum.**

The **House of the Vestal Virgins** and the **Temple of Antonius and Faustina.**

ARCH OF TITUS. — Beautiful triumphal arch built during the reign of Domitian and Trajan to celebrate the victory of Emperor Vespasian and his son Titus over the Jews. During the Middle Ages, the imposing monument was incorporated into the Fortress of Frangipani. Under the pontificate of Pope Sixtus IV it was partly isolated and in 1821 the architect Giuseppe Valadier completely restored it. The architectural ensemble with its single barrel-vault is of very fine proportions. Two celebrated bas-reliefs which represent the triumph of Titus are placed under the intrados of the arch. They are unique works of sculpture executed in the illusionistic technique of the Flavian period.

Another suggestive view of the *Roman Forum*. In the foreground, the remains of the **Temple of Castor and Pollux.** At the right, the Senate-house beside which is the **Church of the Saints Martina and Luca.** In the background the **Arch of Septimius Severus** and the **Column of the Emperor Foca.**

THE BASILICA OF MAXENTIUS OR OF CONSTANTINE. — The grandiose remains of this beautiful basilica which was begun by Maxentius between 306 and 312 and finished by Constantine, constitutes an excellent example of Roman constructive technique. Rectangular in form, divided into three naves with barrel and cross vaults, the imposing basilica served for the administration of justice and civil affairs. What we see is only the right nave of the magnificient construction. For an idea of the size of the original building, it is enough to think that the arcades which have remained until our time measure 20.50 meters in width, 17.50 meters in depth, and 24.50 meters in height.

THE ARCH OF SEPTIMIUS SEVERUS. — The arch celebrates the victories of the Emperor Septimius Severus and his sons Geta and Caracalla in the East. It was constructed in 203 A.D. with three inter-communicating barrel-vaults and is 23 meters high and 25 meters wide. From an architectural point of view its beauty lies in its harmonic proportions. On the smaller barrel-vaults are reliefs representing episodes of the war led by Severus. The excellent preservation of this monument is owed to the fact that during the Middle Ages it was incorporated into other buildings erected as a protection against Roman barons.

A suggestive night view of the *Roman Forum*.

THE IMPERIAL FORUMS

The zone where we now see the ruins of the various Imperial Forums, was occupied by housing of all types during the time of the Roman Republic. These dwellings beseiged the Roman Forum cutting off the possibility of a vaster urbanistic breathing space. Julius Caesar was the first to have the idea of clearing the area of those dwellings substituting them with others more useful to public life. And so we have the Forum of Caesar in 54-46 B.C., the Forum of Augustus in 32-31 B.C., the Forum of Vespasian or Forum of the Peace in 71-75 A.D., the Forum of Nerva in 98 A.D., and last the Forum of Trajan in 113 A.D. which was completed by Emperor Hadrian.

As one can imagine, this complex of buildings was layed out in such a way as to give the entire area a truly monumental

A unique view of the **Forum of Trajan.** At the left the famous column with reliefs dedicated to the undertakings of this Emperor. At the right, the graceful dome of the Church of SS. Nome di Maria.

20

character both from an artistic and from an urbanistic point of view. With the passing of centuries, however, everything fell to ruin. During the mediaeval epoch, a highly populated living quarter developed among the ruins. In the Renaissance the ruins which were still visible of the various forums were pillaged for use in new constructions.

One can say that the rediscovery of the Imperial Forums began with the excavations of 1812-14 when the first vestiges of the Forum of Trajan were brought to light, and again in 1889 during the excavations of the Forum of Caesar.

It was another thirty-four years before a definitive excavation took place. In 1911 the Senator Corrado Ricci presented a project to the government, and in 1924 the enormous job of demolishing the existing ancient housing of the area was undertaken. As a result, the Forums that we admire today were brought to light. Moreover, in 1932-33, under the direction of the architect Antonio Muñoz, the excavation was continued with the discovery of the splendid road of the Imperial Forums. This road which is 850 meters long and 30 meters wide gives us the opportunity of taking one of the most beautiful archeological walks in the world.

A partial panoramic view of Rome showing the white mass of the Victor Emmanuel Monument or the Altar of the Patria, and the beginning of the spectacular Street of the Imperial Forums.

The Markets of Trajan and the Military Tower. The architectural complexity of the Markets of Trajan in all their grandeur can be seen in the semicircular exedra before us. The building, rising in stages, is composed of six floors with a series of windows and doors that were originally shops, since the building was dedicated to commercial affairs. In the center, at the top is the ponderous Military Tower erected on Servian ruins in the thirteenth century by Pope Gregory IX. By popular tradition it is called « Nero's Tower » because it is said that from this point the Emperor assisted in the burning of Rome.

Forum of Augustus. Here are the remains of the beautiful Forum of Augustus built to commemorate the victory of Filippi. Brutus and Cassius, the antagonists of the Emperor and the murderers of Julius Caesar were defeated and perished here. The Forum was dedicated to Marte Ultore from whose temple can be seen a wide stairway and some columns at the bottom of the high wall. Here and there the remains of two basilicas with apses.

The Altar of the Patria, and in the foreground, the remains of the **Forum of Trajan** with the famous column illustrating the undertakings of the Emperor. The column which is in an excellent state of preservation, is composed of eighteen blocks of marble, and is 29.78 meters high. Along the shaft winds a spiral frieze with representations of the warlike exploits of the Emperor against the Dacians. At the top there was once the statue of Trajan, but since 1587 a bronze statue of St. Peter has been placed there. The statue was executed by Tommaso della Porta with the collaboration of Leonardo Sormani.

The Colosseum is the most famous and well-known monument of Roman antiquity. The construction of this enormous Flavian amphitheatre was begun in 72 A.D. by the Emperors of the Flavian family and completed under Titus in 80 A.D. It was destined to be used for gladiatorial contests and wild beast hunts. The origin of its name is not known precisely. Some believe it was given this name because of its gigantic proportions; others say it refers to a colossal statue of Nero which once stood near it.

The Colosseum constitutes a true architectural masterpiece. An elliptical form, it is four storeys high. The first three storeys are arcaded with columns of the Tuscan, Ionic, and Corinthian Orders. The fourth storey or attic is blind, that is, without arcades, but has small rectangular windows. The main axis measures 188 meters, the minor axis 156 meters, the circumference

527 meters, while its greatest height is 57 meters. It was able to hold as many as 50,000 spectators.

Externally, the Colosseum is composed of large Travertine blocks originally secured together by iron cramps which were pillaged during the Middle Ages. Tufa, bricks, and concrete were also used in construction. Little more than half way up the attic, we see numerous brackets which once encircled the entire amphitheatre. They served to support poles which were inserted into

In the photo: To the left, an ideal reconstruction of the exterior of the Colosseum from the part which faces the Arch of Constantine. In the foreground is the conical fountain called the « perspiring » fountain because the water comes out of its exterior like drops of perspiration. To the right is the Colosseum in its actual form after conservative restorations.

special openings placed at the tip of the entablature. The poles, in turn, supported the « velarium » or awning used to protect the spectators from the sun and rain. To manoeuvre this enormous awning required the assistance of a team of sailors from the Fleet of the Misenum. The eighty arcades of the first storey were numbered to regulate the entrance of the public. During the centuries, the hugh mass had undergone notable dammage following earthquakes. It was restored several times but new seismic disasters and other violations brought about its decay. During the Middle Ages and the Renaissance the Palazzo Venezia, the Cancelleria and the Ripetta Gate were constructed with its materials. Finally, in the years 1740-58 Pope Benedict XIV wished to bring an end to the havoc, and declared the Colosseum sacred because according to tradition, the blood of early Christians was spilt in its arena. This tradition has not been historically proven. Since then, other popes had it restored and between 1893-96, the Italian government ordered excavations to isolate the exterior and expose the underground parts.

The interior of the Colosseum must have presented a marvellous view. It was completely covered with marble and the tiers were divided into three large areas: the first was reserved for high-society Romans, the second for the citizens, the third for the common people. Senators and horsemen sat on two or three rows of marble seats in a high podium. Above it stood the Imperial box in which vestal virgins and consuls had the right to enter. In front of the Imperial box, on the opposite side of the amphitheatre, stood the tribune where the prefect of Rome, the magistrates, and the priests were seated. In the upper areas, the citizens were divided

In the photo: To the left, an ideal reconstruction of the interior of the amphitheatre, as it must have been originally. To the right, that which remains of the arena and the tiers.

29

according to the rank and privilege of the various social categories to which they belonged. It seems there was also a clear division of sex; that is, at least for the common people. Men and women watched the spectacle separately.

The enormous arena where the spectacle took place was constructed partly in wood and partly in masonry. It was sprinkled with sand or arranged in some other way depending on the type of representation on the program. In fact, the Romans were extremely fond of gladiatorial combats, the hunting of ferocious beasts, and naval battles. These types of spectacles endured for a long period in the Colosseum, but with the coming of Christianity, events changed and bloody combats were no longer appreciated. So it was that in 404 A.D. the Emperor Honorius prohibited them, however, the hunting of wild beasts continued until the sixth century.

THE UNDERGROUND OF THE COLOSSEUM

The cyclopean walls of the Colosseum give us an impressive example of the building capacity of Roman architects, however, the archeological excavations have revealed to us yet another aspect of their ability. The Romans were able to create highly functional underground environments in relation to the type of spectacle that was being performed

in the arena. We may note (in the two photographs to the left and right) with what building logic the Romans created the underground services. Particular corridors and rooms were reserved to hold ferocious beasts, to make them manageable for their entrance into the arena at the opportune moment. Moreover, in these underground rooms there were manoeuvrable devices in wood and metal necessary for changing scenery and people. All this contributed to the fine success of the spectacle. The Romans were very exacting in the matter. The stagehands paid with their lives for any error which compromised the success of the spectacle.

THE ARCH OF CONSTANTINE. — This unique elegant monument of Roman antiquity tacitly recalls the coming of Christianity. In fact it is dedicated to the Emperor Constantine victor over Maxentius at Ponte Milvio, who with the Edict of Milan in 313 recognized the Christian religion as the pre-eminent religion of the State. The famous arch with three barrel-vaults was dedicated to Constantine by the Roman Senate in 316 A.D. for his victory over Maxentius. During the Middle Ages, its mass was included in the house-fortress of the Frangipane; it was restored in the eighteenth century and again in 1804 as one sees it today. The decorative panels and the statues which adorn it come from other monuments of Roman antiquity; in fact they belong to the monuments of Trajan, Hadrian and Marcus Aurelius. The figures of the Victories, and those of the soldiers and prisoners that can be seen at the base of the columns are from the period of Constantine as are the Victories and the figures of the rivers in the arches, the medallions, and the reliefs in the middle of the arch which refer to the exploits of Constantine.

THE SACRED WAY. — A suggestive and imposing view of the polygonal-shaped flint-stones paving the Sacred Way. It gives us a live example of Roman concreteness. It is called sacred for two reasons: first, Romulus and T. Tazio travelled on it after the pact between Romans and Latins, and second, its route passes among sanctuaries and was the road of processions. In the background is the Arch of Titus.

In the photo: On the right a view of the ruins of the Temple dedicated to **Venus and Roma;** in the background, the bell-tower of the **Church of Santa Francesca Romana;** on the left the **Sacred Way** which leads to the **Arch of Titus.**

THE PALATINE

According to legend, the Palatine is the place where Rome was founded, the city traced out by the tracks of Romulus into the form of a square. Today the Palatine hill appears level ground, but in ancient times there were three hills. These uneven hills were covered with superb Imperial buildings. From the very beginning, the early square-shaped city grew notably larger and in the time of Servio Tullio was enclo-sed within walls. As a consequence of the expansion of the city, the Palatine lost some of its importance, even if it remained the sacred hill of Rome's origin. It was preferred by rich Romans for building their splendid villas and then it became the official residence of the emperors. Political events of the Roman Empire slowly brought about the decadence of the Palatine, although during the barbaric and Byzantine epochs it was

The modern thoroughfare **Way of the Imperial Forums** which leads to Piazza Venezia passing on one side of the Altar of the Patria. To the left a view of the Roman Forum.

the residence of leaders and later of emperors of the Western Empire. In the Middle Ages fortresses of the nobility, churches, convents, and gardens were erected on its famous ruins.

We owe the rediscovery of the Palatine to the systematic archeological investigation which began in the first half of the eighteenth century and has continued to our time thanks to such learned archeologists as P. Rosa, Lanciani, Boni and Romanelli. Excavations have brought to light the ruins of the Temple of Cibele, the House of Livia, the Criptoporticus of Nero, the Flavian Palace, the Domus Augustana, official residence of the Emperors, the Palace of Septimius Severus, the Settizonio, the Stadium of Domitian, the Lupercalia, the houses of Tiberius and Caligula, the Temple of Jove Statore and that of Venus and Rome.

THE TEMPLE OF VESTA AT THE BOARIO FORUM. — We know another Temple of Vesta in the Roman Forum. The one we see here has assumed the same name because of its similar circular form; however, it has nothing to do with the worship of Vesta. It seems that it was dedicated to Portumnus, divinity of the river gate, or to the Sun God. This very beautiful pagan temple rose in the first century of the Empire. The circle of Corinthian columns encloses a cylindrical cell constructed in white marble blocks. The building is incomplete since the pediment and the original roofing have been lost. During the Middle Ages it was dedicated to Santa Maria del Sole.

THE MARCELLO THEATRE. — A picturesque view of the Marcello Theatre with the three columns belonging to an angle of the Temple of Apollo Sosiano on the right. The conspicuous ruins of the theatre have become the supporting structure of the Orsini Palace designed by Baldassarre Peruzzi in 1500. However, the imposing construction was begun by Julius Caesar, and brought to a conclusion by Augustus in 13-11 B.C. who dedicated it to the memory of his nephew Marco Claudio Marcello. Alberto Calza Bini executed the restoration of the lower order of arches in 1926-29. The theatre had a capacity to hold ten thousand spectators. Using some of the material of this theatre, the Ponte Cestio was restored in 365-70.

The Arch of Giano dates from the period between Diocletian and Constantine. It is an unusual monument that was greatly admired by Renaissance artists. It was dedicated to Giano Quadrifronte; the name derives from « janus », a word used by the Romans to describe covered passageways leading in four directions. In the Middle Ages, it became part of the Fortress of Frangipane.

The Temple of Fortuna Virile is one of the most unusual and well-preserved monuments of Roman antiquity. It dates from the period between 100-80 B.C. Its denomination is not exact; it seems to have been originally dedicated to the Mater Matuta. It is in a Greco-Italian style. In 872 it was transformed into a Christian church dedicated to Santa Maria Egiziaca.

39

The Pyramid of Caius Cestius is found immediately outside the Porta San Paolo. Its geometric shape makes us think of far away Egyptian monuments, however, it is none other than the tomb of Caius Cestius, magistrate and tribune of the people. Constructed in 12 B.C., it is 27 meters high and has a base 22 meters wide on each side. It is covered with Lunense marble which bears an inscription telling us it was built in three hundred and thirty days.

Porta San Sebastiano is one of the most beautiful gates of Rome included in the Aurelian walls. In ancient times it was called the Appian Gate. It was reconstructed by Onorio in the fifth century, and restored by Narsete and Belisario in the sixth century. Flanked externally by two imposing towers, it constitutes a rare example of antique fortification.

THE TOMB OF CECILIA METELLA
is a sepulchral monument on the antique
Appian Way dedicated to the wife of Crasso,
son of the famous triumvir. It has a cylindrical form and a diameter measuring 20
meters. At the top there is a fine frieze.
During the Middle Ages it was transformed
into a crenelated tower and incorporated
into the adjacent castle which belonged to
the Counts of Tuscolo. The unusual sepulchral monument dates back to the last
decade of the Roman Republic.

THE ANTIQUE APPIAN WAY begins
just beyond the Porta San Sebastiano. It was
constructed by Appio Claudio in 312 B.C.
who at first extended it as far as Capua and
later to Brindisi and Taranto. The great con-
sular road which here and there conserves
traces of the original pavement, presents us
with an impressive sequence of tombs, and
of Roman ruins; it is further enhanced by the
landscape which surrounds it.

MONUMENTAL ROME

(Palaces, Squares, Fountains and Monuments)

Archeology has revealed the face of ancient Rome to us. Now we need to follow historical events to learn about the formation of the new city which rose on the ruins of the Western Empire, after it had undergone the irreparable attacks of the barbarians. These attacks had decreased the population, and brought about its decay from an urbanistic and political point of view. The gradual assertion of temporal power by the Catholic Church was the remedy for the rebirth of the city. If there were some preliminary difficulties, after the year one thousand, and for almost three centuries, the aspect of the city presented itself to the visitor as a city-fortress. It was composed of numerous towers and palaces constructed for the offense and defense of the nobility who were divided into various factions continuously fighting each other.

It was not until the return of the Popes

PIAZZA NAVONA. — The most outstanding square of the Baroque period in Rome. It has the same shape and size as the Domitian Stadium. *In the photo on the right*: In the foreground the Fountain of the Moors; to the left the Church of Saint Agnes in Agony begun by Francesco Borromini (1652-57). *In the photo below*: The famous fountain by Bernini called **The Rivers.**

from their captivity in Avignon, that we see the reestablishment of harmony among the citizens, and consequently, the beginning of a lasting urbanistic settlement. Under Pope Sixtus IV, a real building program was put into effect with the construction of new churches and palaces to which the architects, painters, and sculptors of the fifteenth century gave the best of their genius. In the sixteenth century Bramante, Michelangelo, Antonio da Sangallo the Younger and Domenico Fontana interpreted very well the directions of Paul III and Sixtus V. They gave the city that façade which we admire today in all its majesty, not only for the layout of roads, but also for the construction of new imposing basilicas, grandiose palaces, and beautiful suburban villas.

Two very great architects of the seventeenth century contributed in an essential way in making the unusual face of the city still more splendid: Gian Lorenzo Bernini and Francesco Borromini. They displayed fervid building activity, populating the roads and Roman squares with noble Baroque buildings. It is enough to think that during the period of their ingenious activity the Palaces Doria, Montecitorio, Barberini, Mattei, Altieri, Pamphili, and part of Propaganda Fide were built; also the twin churches of Piazza del Popolo, the oratory of Filippini, the belfry and apse of Sant'Andrea delle Fratte, Sant' Ivo della Sapienza, the little Church of San Carlino, and the very beautiful Bernini Fountains.

One can not say that the eighteenth century contributed to the city in an urbanistic sense. In that century the quarters between the Corso and the Via del Babuino and the Northern Campo Marzo were built. A large quantity of housing was layed out in such a confused way that it compromised the urbanistic future of a vast zone of the city. However, aside from its defects, the eighteenth century also left its imprint with the construction of the very beautiful steps to Trinità dei Monti, the new façade of the Basilica of Santa Maria Maggiore, San Giovanni in Lateran, the famous Trevi Fountain, and the Palaces Braschi, Corsini and della Consulta.

In the nineteenth century, tired of Baroque and Rococco, Rome indulged in a neoclassicism which echoed the Greek architectural orders and Roman Imperial architecture. It declined to a rather cold and irritating conventionalism, however, it was in this period that several new innovations took place: the layout of Piazza del Popolo by Giuseppe Valadier, and the opening of new roads such as Via Merulana, Via San Giovanni, and Via Viminale. Archeological excavations were begun in the Roman and Trajan Forums, as well as the restoration of several

THE VITTORIANO. — Located on the slope of the Capitoline Hill this grandiose monument celebrates Italian independence. It is certainly not in harmony with the atmosphere created in the past by the artists and urbanists for the Eternal city. Nevertheless, it is an expression and a seal of the epoch of the Risorgimento and of artistic taste at the end of the nineteenth century. Inspired by Hellenistic forms in its slightly curvilinear arcade, it is flanked by propylaea on which are displayed the chariots symbolic of the unity and liberty of Italy. In the center is the equestrian statue of King Vittorio Emanuele II; in the projection below, the sculpture of the Goddess Roma, and in the interior of the altar the tomb of the Unknown Soldier. In front, the large ascending stairway and two groups in gilded bronze which represent (on the left) « Thought » and (on the right) « Action ». The works were begun in 1885 by Giuseppe Sacconi and were finished in 1911. *In the photo below*: The equestrian statue of King Vittorio Emanuele II, work of the sculptor Enrico Chiaradia, executed between 1888 and 1901 in gilded bronze. It measures 12 meters in length and the same in height.

monuments of antiquity. Rome, having become the capital of Italy, underwent the imposition of development programs which did not take into account the future growth of the city. In this period rose the new quarters on the Esquiline, on the Celio, beyond the Tiber, as well as the seat of the Ministry, the Monument to Vittorio Emanuele II, the Palaces of Justice, of Exhibitions, of the Bank of Italy, and of Queen Margherita. This latter was by the architect Gaetano Koch, to whom we also owe the intelligent layout of Piazza dell'Esedra. At the beginning of the twentieth century, the imposing buildings destined to become the seats of various ministries and public corporations were constructed. In the period between the two world wars the city was enriched by new churches, convents, hospitals, and bridges over the Tiber. At the same time, we see a growth both to the north and to the east of an urban agglomeration.

Palazzo Venezia: the plan of this great palace is attributed to Leon Battista Alberti. It is the first work of the Renaissance in Rome (1455-67). Elegant, harmonious, and imposing, it was the residence of the Popes until 1564, and then of the ambassadors from the Republic of Venice. One should note the beautiful cross-shaped windows on the first floor and the characteristic Guelf crenelations completing the structure.

The steep stairway which leads up to the **Church of Santa Maria d'Aracoeli,** constructed in 1348. On the right the steps leading up to the **Piazza del Campidoglio.**

THE CAMPIDOGLIO. — This has been the most important hill in Rome since the origins of the city. It was the religious and political center of the ancient Roman people as it is today the center of civic administration in Rome. The beautiful square is an urbanistic masterpiece by Michelangelo Buonarroti. Having climbed the wide stairway, guarded on both sides by the divine Dioscuri Castor and Pollux, one arrives in front of the equestrian statue of the Emperor Marcus Aurelius. The statue is immediately behind the Palace of the Senate, the municipal center with its high tower from where one may enjoy a vast panorama of the city. To the right is the Palace of the Conservatori and on the left the Capitoline Museum.

The Campidoglio. — The beautiful bronze equestrian statue of the Imperial Age (originally gilded) of the Emperor Marcus Aurelius. Michelangelo wished to have it in the Piazza del Campidoglio, and had it transported there from the Lateran.

THE QUIRINAL PALACE. — It rises on the highest of the Roman hills where in ancient times the Sanctuary of Quirino existed for which the hill and the palace are named. At first it was the residence of the Popes, after 1870 it received the Sovereigns of Italy, and from 1947 it has been the official residence of the President of the Italian Republic. Pope Gregory XIII began its construction in 1574 and it was completed in 1730-40 under the direction of famous architects. In the course of almost two centuries, Mascherino, Domenico Fontana, Flaminio Ponzio, Carlo Maderno, Gian Lorenzo Bernini and Ferdinando Fuga worked on it. Its late Renaissance façade is divided into two levels; the doorway is by Maderno. To the left, a detail of the beautiful Fountain of the Dioscuri.

THE TREVI FOUNTAIN. — This is the masterpiece of the Roman architect Nicolò Salvi who was commissioned by the Florentine Pope Clement XII to systematize the already existing spring called *Virgin Water*. This name comes to us from an ancient tradition which tells about a young girl who showed the spring to some thirsty Roman soldiers. In 19 B.C. this water was brought to Rome by Agrippa. He constructed an aquaduct twenty kilometers long to provide for his thermal baths. Salvi knew how to intelligently make use of the existing architecture of the minor façade of the Palace of the Poli Dukes. He produced this scenographic fountain, turning to the Roman sculptor Pietro Bracci for the mythical figuration. The fountain was finished in 1762, and was called Trevi because it was constructed at a point where three roads join together. Italians and foreigners, following the local tradition, throw a coin into the fountain which has the virtue of ensuring their return to Rome.

A panoramic view illustrating some Roman domes. To the left the **Church of Santo Nome di Maria**, then **Santa Maria di Loreto, Gesù** and **Sant'Andrea della Valle**; to the right **Sant'Ivo, San Giovanni dei Fiorentini, Sant'Agnese** and **San Pietro**.

THE TRINITÀ DEI MONTI. — Here is another beautiful view of Rome from the Piazza di Spagna. In the foreground the fountain called « la Barcaccia » or « old boat », a work of the Florentine Pietro Bernini, father of Gian Lorenzo. Behind it, the famous stairway in travertine designed by Alessandro Specchi and Francesco de Sanctis (1723-26). Above, the Piazza Trinità dei Monti with the obelisk which originally came from the Sallustiani Gardens. The church of the same name was begun in 1502 at the wish of King Louis XII of France. It was restored in the nineteenth century by Francesco Mazois.

Piazza della Repubblica (previously Exedra). — One of the most beautiful Roman piazzas dating from the end of the nineteenth century. It is built upon the main exedra of the Baths of Diocletian. The two palaces to the right and left of the Via Nazionale are works of the architect Gaetano Koch who also systematized the piazza. At the center, the *Fountain of the Water Nymphs* decorated with four groups of female figures in bronze and a central group which represents « man victorious over the ugly forces of nature », a work of the sculptor from Palermo Mario Rutelli.

In **Piazza Barberini** this lovely fountain has been admired since 1640. It is called **Triton** and was conceived by Gian Lorenzo Bernini. An open shell, supported by four dolphins, holds up the triton who puffs on a bugle-horn making a jet of water gush out.

Via Vittorio Veneto. — Beautiful palaces, luxurious hotels, and elegant shops have made this wide, modern tree-lined thoroughfare the meeting place of the Roman aristocracy since the beginning of the century. Night and day, the most celebrated personalities of the political, cultural, and artistic world arrange to meet here. Via Veneto is the drawing-room of Rome where the moods of the great city pleasantly oscillate between the serious and the witty; where the quick rhythm of fashion and the birth and decline of celebrities in every field manifests itself; it is where one may feel every phase of the rhythm of the Eternal city.

Villa Borghese: The largest and most beautiful public park in Rome, measuring a perimeter of six kilometers. It constitutes the area around the famous villa by the same name, constructed at the beginning of the seventeenth century for Cardinal Scipione Caffarelli Borghese, nephew of Pope Paul V. Villa and park were purchased in 1902 by the King of Italy who gave it as a gift to the city changing its name to Villa Umberto I; however, the people have continued to call it by its original name. In the photograph, a small lake in the park with an island which has an imitation Greek temple dedicated to Esculapio, designed by architect Antonio Asprucci (1787).

In the center of **Piazza Mattei** one comes across this charming **Fountain of the Turtles,** a magnificent work of the late Renaissance designed by Giacomo della Porta and executed by Taddeo Landini between 1581 and 1584. Four nude figures in bronze induce the turtles to drink from the fountain above. The intertwining of the human figures and the dolphins, and the work as a whole, give us a composition of movement and incomparable grace.

THE PANTHEON. — After the Colosseum this is the most interesting and best preserved monument of Augustan Rome. It was constructed by the son-in-law of Augustus, Marco Agrippa, at the time of his third consulship, as is indicated in the Latin inscription of the pronaos (27 B.C.). It is dedicated to the seven planetary divinities and is called Pantheon which signifies « holiest » or « most sacred temple ». It is beautiful for the architectural conception of its circular plan and for the knowledgeable building technique used in the construction of the dome. The Pantheon is admirable for its grandeur of line and the harmony of its parts. Inside are found the tombs of Italian kings and of the great Raphael.

Photo low down: an interior view of the **Pantheon:** the grandiose space is dominated by the miraculous vault from which the light descends to lay stress on every architectural element

The charming **Fountain of the Small Ship** reproduces a model of a Roman ship. It is found in a square by the same name in front of the Church Santa Maria in Domnica.

The « **Chick of Minerva** » so-called jokingly by the Roman people. This curious monument was created by Gian Lorenzo Bernini and executed by Ercole Ferrata in 1667. The lovely base supports a small marble elephant which in turn supports an Egyptian obelisk of the sixth century B.C. The work is found in **Piazza della Minerva.** Here we see it with the circular walls of the Pantheon behind it.

GENTE
RIAVE GIOIA
Momento-sera
IL TEMPO

The Portico of Octavia. — An interesting view of the
remains of the Portico of Octavia, built in 149 B.C. by
Quinto Metello the Macedonian. It was then reconstructed
by Augustus and dedicated to his sister Octavia. The
remains form an impressive atrium for the Church San-
t'Angelo in Pescheria. Around the portico and in the
adjacent area are living Israelites who have been present
in Rome since the epoch of Pompeus Magnus. It is here
in the vicinity of the **Church of Santa Maria del Pianto**
and along the Tiber that the antique *ghetto* once existed.
It is where the descendents of the noble Hebrew nation
were constrained to live from the sixteenth to the nineteenth centuries.

Between the Via Portico
d'Ottavia and the Lungotevere dei Cenci stands the
Israelite Temple. It is an
imposing structure with a
pavilion dome and an architecture inspired by Assyrian-
Babylonian style. It was designed by the architects Osval-
do Armanni and Costa in
1904.

Along the **Lungotevere Prati** we see the principal façade of the imposing **Palace of Justice,** decorated with statues of the famous jurisprudents. The grandiose building was designed by architect Guglielmo Calderini of Perugia between 1899 and 1910.

The Tiberina Island and the **Fabricio Bridge** which joins the island to Lungotevere dei Cenci. The bridge was constructed by the Consul L. Fabricio in 62 B.C.
It is therefore the most antique bridge in Rome and it is in an excellent state
of preservation.

Piazza Colonna. — Along the Corso we find this beautiful square. It is another meeting place for Roman citizens, especially political men. At the center of the square is the famous **Column of Marcus Aurelius.** Like the Column of Trajan, it is decorated with a spiral showing episodes of the warlike exploits of the Emperor. Erected between 176 and 193 A.D., it is almost 42 meters high including its base. Since 1589 a bronze statue of St Paul has been placed at its top. The statue is attributed to the sculptor Tommaso della Porta. The circular fountain in the foreground is by Giacomo della Porta (1575).

CASTEL SANT'ANGELO. — It is one of the most historically significant monuments in Rome. Originally, it did not have the aspect of a fortress, but of a mausoleum which the Emperor Hadrian planned as a sepulcre for himself and his successors. The mausoleum, which consisted of a large square base to support a cylindrical construction, was begun in 135 A.D. and completed under the Emperor Antonius Pius in 139 A.D. It is perhaps the work of the architect Demetriano. In 271 A.D. the Emperor Aurelianus constructed a new boundary wall across the Tiber and from then on the funerary monument began to assume the aspect of a real fortress. Later, under Theodoric, it was turned into a prison and it continued to function as a defensive rampart disputed by the various factions of the late Middle Ages; it was a safe refuge for popes during civic unrest and warlike invasions; and it was a place of torture, prison, and death not only for habitual delinquents, but also for illustrious political, religious, artistic, and literary personalities.

Its architectural structure has undergone changes over the centuries, internally and externally, under Popes Benedict IX, Nicholas V, Alexander VI, Julius II, Urban the VIII and others. During the Risorgimento patriots were imprisoned there who plotted against the temporal power of the popes. With the unity of Italy it continued as a prison and a fortress, until 1901, when thanks to General Mariano Borgatti, a complete restoration was undertaken. The monument is named after the bronze angel located at its top, which according to religious tradition, was seen in a vision by Pope Gregory the Great, in the act of sheathing its sword, a gesture which indicated the end of the plague.

In **Castel Sant'Angelo** is the courtyard of honor, also called courtyard dell'angelo because of the presence of the sculpture by Raffaello da Montelupo which was once placed at the top of the fortress. At the two sides is ammunition for catapults in marble and travertine.

Castel Sant'Angelo: The angel with unfolded wings who sheaths his sword is a work in bronze by the Belgian sculptor Pietro van Verschaffelt (1752). Since the time of Pope Gregory the Great there have been many sculptures of the angel substituted because of deterioration. The most recent one has been replaced by the marble statue by Giacomo della Porta.

A view of the Tiber near the Vatican: In the foreground, the **Ponte Sant'Angelo** built by the Emperor Hadrian in 136 A.D.; in the background the dome of **St. Peter's.**

Via della Conciliazione. — Before 1936, one arrived in St. Peter's square by following two very beautiful roads called Borgo Vecchio and Borgo Nuovo which formed the well-known « Spina dei Borghi ». The visitor arrived unexpectedly in front of the large square receiving an unforgettable impression. The necessity of directing thousands of faithful from every nation to the greatest Christian basilica has led to today's urbanistic solution, the realization of the plan by architects Marcello Piacentini and Attilio Spaccarelli. The new wide road was finished in 1950. Some buildings, important from an artistic and historical point of view, may be seen along its course.

THE VATICAN

The historical events which led to Italian independence and to the consequent occupation of Rome as natural capital of the new state, caused the temporal power of the papacy to decline after a millennium of life. The Pope, who was then Pius IX, did not recognize the Law of Guarantigie which regulated the relations of the new state independent of the Catholic Church. He shut himself up in the Vatican as a prisoner. Similar attitudes were assumed also by his successors. Finally, on February 11, 1929, Pope Pius XI brought an end to the disagreement with the Italian government in the Treaty of the Lateran. He created the smallest state in the world. This state sanctioned the temporal power of the popes, and allowed the Catholic Church maximum liberty and absolute independence. Without this, the Roman papacy would not have been able to continue its high universal mission.

It was in this way that the Vatican State

was created; an independent state with the pope as absolute head. He became the head of the Catholic Church, Universal Bishop and Bishop of Rome. The Italian government also allowed the Vatican State the privilege of extraterritorial rights. In its numerous properties located all over Rome, the Vatican maintains the indispensible offices which keep the apostolic activity functioning for the spiritual well-being of Christianity. The city rises on the Vatican Hill. The origin of its name is uncertain. « Vaticanum », like « Ianicolum », seems to indicate an Etruscan locality. According to the opinion of the scholar G. B. Niebuhr the locality in very ancient times must have been a village with the name « Vaticum ». From that name derived the adjective « Vatican ». Varrone says the etymology of the word Vatican derives from « Vagitano » which, according to him, was the god who protected the crying of the newborn. Perhaps the first version is the more reliable one. The territory of the Papal State covers the area of the ancient « Ager Vaticanus ». This is where Nero had his gardens which became so famous during the persecution of the Christians. It was here that they underwent tremendous tortures to demonstrate to the pagan world the evangelical truths.

After Christianity was recognized by Constantine the Great, the first basilica dedicated to St. Peter was built on this site. Around it were crowded other constructions of a religious and civil character. Pope Leo IV, in order to defend the basilica which contained the tomb of the Prince of the Apostles from bloody political battles, had the whole area surrounded by a robust wall forming the so-called « Lion City » (848-52). In the course of centuries, other popes added new walls to the first one. The actual Vatican State is almost totally enclosed by a belt of walls constructed between 1550 and 1640 by Popes Paul III, Pius V, and Urban VIII.

The Vatican territory covers an area of 440 thousand square meters. It has the form of a trapezium with the longest side to the south. Its greatest width is little over a thousand meters with a length of 850 meters. Regarding its altimetry, it is nineteen meters above sea level in St. Peter's Square, 77.5 in the Vatican Gardens, and at the north-west wall measures 56.5. Of the entire area which covers 44 hectares, 55 thousand square meters are occupied by various offices, and the rest is composed of gardens and building plots. The confines of the Vatican are determined by the surrounding wall and by the part of St. Peters Square where a strip of travertine marble marks the pavement. Here, the two arms of Bernini's colonnade join together. They enclose a space which goes back as far as the Arch of the Campane, the gates of the basilica, and the Bronze Doorway.

The population of the Vatican does not exceed one thousand. As is suited to a sovereign state, it possesses every requisite: it is run by a civil authority and judicial body, it stamps its own money, issues stamps, and is distinguished by a flag (yellow and white with the papal coat-of-arms). It possesses armed troops which more than anything else have the function of vigilance and honor. There is an electric power station, a radio transmitting and receiving station, and a railway station. It also keeps diplomatic representatives in almost every country of the world.

For the smooth functioning of the various services and state organs, the position of Governor was created. It is he who watches over such offices as: postal, telegraph, telephone, philatelic, the general direction of monuments, technical and economic services,

THE APOSTOLIC PALACE. — Looking at the façade of the basilica, one may see the Apostolic Palace to its right, beyond Bernini's column. On the top floor is the private apartment of the Pope. The second window from the right is where he appears on Sunday to bless the faithful crowd in the square. The Apostolic Palace is a vast complex of rooms where the Pope lives and works and where the Vatican Museum is also found. The multiple structures of which it is composed have been built slowly during the centuries according to the wishes of various popes.

A spectacular view of marvellous **St. Peter's Square.** The basilica, Bernini's porticoes, and the Apostolic Palace seen in one wide-angle photograph.

the civil state, the legal office, and the notary section. The governor is assisted by the Councillor General of the State, selected by the pope; there is also a penal and civil court which, along with two special commissions, examines civil and ecclesiastic cases. Since there are no shops in the Vatican, a provisions department was formed to provide for all the needs of the population, and to look after the functioning of hygenic and sanitary services.

ST. PETER'S SQUARE

It is not an exaggeration of we define this square as the most beautiful in the world. We owe it to the great architectural genius of the Neopolitan Gian Lorenzo Bernini, son of the Florentine sculptor Pietro Bernini. He created a truc masterpiece with the two immense semicircles that relate so well with the trapezoidal space in front of the façade of the basilica. The colonnade of Bernini was built between 1656 and 1667. It is composed of two hundred and eighty four imposing columns in the Doric order and eighty-eight pilasters. The columns are arranged in four rows forming three covered ambulatories which altogether measure seventeen meters in width. The colonnade is nineteen meters high; it encloses an area 148 meters wide and 198 meters long. It is surmounted by a beautiful entablature with balustrade on which ninety-six statues representing saints and martyrs stand out. They are 3.20 meters high. They were sculpted by pupils of Bernini but the master furnished the drawings for many of them. Approaching the square, it is possible to admire the grandiose effect of the entire scene, including the façade of the basilica, the marvellous dome of Michelangelo, the obelisk and the two fountains. The impression we receive is somewhat disconcerting because of the gigantic proportions of every element, particularly Bernini's colonnade outstretched towards us, as if to receive everything in a single affectionate embrace. And in fact this was the intent of the genius Bernini; to make us understand indelibly the maternal greatness of the Catholic Church, ready to embrace all people of every race and color in a single stroke of charity and love. This incomparable vision prepares us to understand better the harmonious vastness of the basilica.

THE BASILICA OF ST. PETER

For those who want to have an immediate understanding of Michelangelo's ingenious architectural conception, it is necessary to ascend to the level of the third pilasters. From this point, the dome and the three apses may be admired in all their splendour in a single breathtaking view. The present basilica replaced an earlier one founded by Constantine the Great between 324 and 349. Its foundation stone was blessed by Pope Julius II on April 18, 1506. The first architect to work on it was Bramante, and in time there followed Raffaello, Fra Giocondo, Giuliano da Sangallo, Antonio da Sangallo the Elder, and Baldassarre Peruzzi; however these architects contributed very little. Those who were really active in its construction were the Florentine Antonio da Sangallo the Younger, followed by Michelangelo Buonarroti, Domenico Fontana, Giacomo della Porta and Carlo Maderno.

The basilica was consecrated by the Florentine Pope Urban VIII on November 18, 1626. It covers a surface of more than a hectare and a half, is 211.50 meters long including the portico and the thickness of the walls, and is 141.50 meters high.

A partial view of **St. Peter's Square.** In the foreground the fountain designed by Carlo Maderno. In the background the central part of the façade of the basilica designed by the same architect. He finished it in 1614 after seven years' work.

THE INTERIOR OF THE BASILICA OF
ST. PETER

The colossal proportions of St. Peter's Square and of all its architectural elements and sculpture have already prepared us to understand the enormous vastness of the basilica. The over-all harmony of the interior composed of so many uniquely proportioned parts, is difficult to perceive immediately. To understand it better we should use as our point of reference the two holy water fonts located at the sides of the central nave.

At first sight, they appear to be a normal size, but if we draw closer to them we notice at once their enormous proportions. The central nave is a vault with white and gold coffering. It is forty-six meters high and twenty-seven meters wide. It is separated from the side naves by eight enormous pilasters flanked by minor pilasters which sustain the arches.

St. Peter's Chair. We find ourselves in front of another masterpiece by Gian Lorenzo Bernini. The artist has framed the Apostle's chair in gilded bronze weighed from above in a circumfusion of luminous clouds with two angels at the sides. Above, we find the symbol of the Holy Spirit, the white dove, enclosed in a halo of rays of revolving angels. Below, at the sides, are four Doctors of the Church.

The Baldacchino by Bernini. Another marvellous view of the interior of St. Peter's. In the foreground the gigantic « baldacchino » in bronze which encloses the Papal altar. It was conceived by Bernini when he was only twenty-six years old, in the most pure and imaginative Baroque style. One can see that the colossal proportions do not diminish the architectural lines which surround it. The monumental and elegant work was ordered by the Florentine Pope Urban VIII Barbarini, who intuited the artistic genius of Bernini and was his greatest patron.

Michelangelo: « Pietà ». This sculptural masterpiece by Michelangelo was ordered by the French Cardinal Di Lagraulas for his tomb in 1498. The artist created it when he was only twenty-five years old. The group has been created with a gentleness and dignity of line. Above all, the calm resigned suffering of the youthful Virgin and the abandon of Christ's body, strike us. It does not have the rigidity of death but seems drowsy with a sleep which preludes His resurrection.

Bronze statue of St. Peter. This work was once believed to be created in the fifth century, but modern critics seem to agree on a more recent dating. Probably it was executed in the thirteenth century by Arnolfo di Cambio. This image of the Prince of the Apostles has always been venerated in the course of centuries. The right foot is worn away by the kisses of millions of faithful.

IOANNES P.P. XXIII

The Dome viewed from the « baldacchino ». The interior of Michelangelo's immense dome is divided into 16 ribs with the same number of windows. The diameter measures 42 meters.

The Tomb of Pope John XXIII. In the Holy Grottoes, situated in the subterranean part of the Vatican basilica, the tomb of Pope John XXIII is the goal of pilgrimages by the faithful from all over the world. It was this Pope who announced the Ecumenical Council, Vatican II which has had such a profound effect on all Chritianity.

The Arch of the Campane and the Swiss Guards. — It is one of the four entrances to the Vatican City, situated to the left of St. Peter's Basilica. From here, one passes for a visit to the Papal State and to the Holy Grottoes. At the sides of the entrance are two soldiers of the Swiss Guard in sixteenth century costume. This armed papal guard was founded by Pope Julius II in 1506. The magnificent uniform seems to have been designed by Michelangelo and Raphael. It is called Swiss because its soldiers came and even now are recruited from Catholic citizens of Swiss nationality.

The Dome of St. Peter's. Constructed from a drawing by Michelangelo which was inspired by the dome of Santa Maria del Fiore in Florence.

THE SISTINE CHAPEL

Between 1475 and 1483, Pope Sixtus IV employed the Florentine architect Giovannino de' Dolci to construct the ceiling. At that time it was to serve two purposes, liturgical and defensive. The interior is 40.23 meters long, 13.41 meters wide, and 20.73 meters high. The walls are decorated with very beautiful frescoes by famous Tuscan and Umbrian masters. But the greatest attraction of the Sistine Chapel is the marvellous picture cycle by Michelangelo which begins with the decoration of the enormous vault (almost 520 square meters). It narrates different episodes of the Creation of the Universe, of Man, Original Sin, the Flood, the Rebirth of Man, and it ends with the masterpiece frescoed on the walls of the altar (200 square meters of surface) narrating the theme « Universal Judgement ». The vault was frescoed between 1508 and 1512, the walls twenty-three years later, between 1535 and 1541.

THE FRESCOES OF THE VAULT

1. THE CREATION OF MAN
2. ORIGINAL SIN AND EXPULSION FROM PARADISE
3. THE CREATION OF WOMAN
4. GOD DIVIDING LIGHT FROM DARKNESS
5. THE FRESCOES OF THE VAULT
6. LIBYAN SIBYL
7. THE PROPHET DANIEL
8. THE PROPHET ISAIAH
9. DELPHIC SIBYL
10. CUMEAN SIBYL
11. ERYTHRAEAN SIBYL
12. THE PROPHET ZACHARIAH
13. THE PROPHET EZEKIEL

THE LAST JUDGEMENT (Sistine Ceiling)

14. DETAIL OF THE LAST JUDGEMENT
15. THE LAST JUDGEMENT
16. DETAIL OF CHRIST THE JUDGE

Les photos n. 2, 3, 4, 5, 6, 7, 8, 9, 10, 11, 12, 13, 14, sont de Bruno del Priore - Rome
Les Photos n. 1, 15, 16, sont de la Maison Scala - Florence

LIBICA

DANIEL

ESAIAS

DELPHICA

CVMAEA

E Z E C H I E L

3

5

St. Peters Square and **Via della Concilia-zione** in a beautiful photographic view taken from the dome. Underneath: the **Palazzo del Governatorato.**

CHURCHES AND BASILICAS

It would not be possible in a publication of this size to present a photographic view of all the churches and basilicas in Rome. One must remember that the Eternal City, being the very center of Christianity, has two hundred and ninety-three churches and seven large basilicas. We will cite only those churches and basilicas which are most frequented by tourists and by the faithful who gather here from every part of the world.

However, if we are unable to present every religious building which from an archeological, architectural, sculptural, and pictorial point of view deserves to be mentioned, at least we can give a brief historical outline of their construction. Christian architecture began in Rome after the famous Edict of Constantine in 313. There are two different types of construction found repeatedly in the local tradition: the longitudinal or basilical system which is a pure Roman conception, and the centralized or round system.

At the beginning, the Christian basilica was composed of a large open quadrangular atrium with arcades on three or four sides. The interior contained from three to five naves, while the smaller churches had only a single nave. The central nave led into a semi-circular opening with a hemispherical covering called an apse. The ceilings, supported by walls built on rows of columns and pilasters, were almost always trussed, often painted, or hidden by coffering.

The longitudinal type basilica was found in Rome in the fourth and fifth centuries: for example, the first basilica of St. Peter's in the Vatican, rebuilt during the Renaissance; St. Paul Outside the Walls, destroyed in a fire and rebuilt in the nineteenth century; San Giovanni in Lateran, reconstructed in the seventeenth century; and Santa Maria Maggiore which, in general line, together with the Basilica of Santa Sabina, has preserved its original aspect.

For examples of basilicas with the round or circular plan and the domed roof, we shall cite the Church of Santa Costanza, Santo Stefano Rotondo, and the Baptistry of San Giovanni ad Fontes near the Basilica of San Giovanni in Lateran. Often this type of construction was preferred for a baptistry by neophythe Christians.

In the Byzantine period, the basilical system was still used with the difference that the apse was no longer semicircular, but polygonal. In the centrally planned churches, they preferred to develop a square, circular, octagonal, or Greek cross construction with a domed roof. However, in Rome, Byzantine architecture did not have a following. Traces of it may be seen in the Churches of San Lorenzo and Sant'Agnese Outside the Walls, built in the seventh century.

SANTA MARIA MAGGIORE. Flanked by two palaces of equal size, the principal façade of the basilica is a true architectural jewel by the Florentine architect Ferdinando Fuga who built it between 1743 and 1750. On the right rises the Romanesque style bell tower which is the highest in Rome. In the foregrund, in the middle of Piazza Santa Maria Maggiore, is the beautiful Roman column which came from the Basilica of Maxentius and was placed there in 1614. It is surmounted by the bronze statue of the *Madonna and Child* by Guglielmo Berthelot.

From the eighth century until the year one thousand, the churches echoed oriental themes, as one can see in the Churches of Santa Maria in Domnica, Santa Prassede and Santa Maria in Aracoeli. During the period in which Romanesque art flourished from the tenth to the twelfth centuries, there came about an elaboration of various artistic elements which repeated Roman and Byzantine motifs. Churches were constructed with slightly inclined roofs, hemispherical arches turned on columns, cross and barrel vaults, polyhedral domes, cruciform and composite pilasters, heavy buttresses, and narrow windows. Also, in this epoch there is a renewal of interest in the decorative elements of Paleo-Christian basilicas. Families of marble workers such a Cosmati and Vassalletto used their polychromed inlaid marbles as an integral part of the architecture. This may be seen in the basilicas of Santa Maria in Trastevere, San Clemente, and Santa Maria in Cosmedin.

The advent of Gothic architecture — preferring the cross vault and reducing the essential part of construction to a framework of pilasters, ribs, vaults, and pointed arches — did not have much fortune in Rome. In fact there is only one example of this style of architecture in the Church of Santa Maria Sopra Minerva, which was erected on the ruins of the Temple of Minerva Calcidicia by the Domenican architects Fra Sisto and Fra Ristoro of Florence in 1280.

The same must be said for Renaissance architecture and the concepts of Alberti and Laurana who were directed to studies of the movement of monumental masses and to the free disposition of forms in space and in relation to it. Religious buildings in the Renaissance style are San Cosimato, Santa Maria del Popolo, the façade of Santa Maria Sopra Minerva, Sant'Agostino, and St. Peter in Chains. In the sixteenth century, Renaissance architecture assumes the characteristics of rhythmic beauty, spacial amplitude, and vigorous effects obtained by the grouping of lines and volumes. Built in this century are the Church of San Pietro in Montorio, the Basilica of St. Peter's, Sant'Eligio degli Orefici, Santa Maria di Loreto, Santo Spirito in Sassia, Santa Maria degli Angeli, the Church of Gesù, the Church of Sant'Andrea, and the façade of the Church of San Luigi dei Francesi.

Baroque architecture, which developed in the seventeenth century, was dedicated to studies of new and unusual effects, the play of light and shadow, the glorification of the grandiose and of sumptuous decoration. It has a rich representation in Rome; for example in the Church of San Salvatore in Lauro, the façade of Sant'Eligio degli Orefici, the Church of San Sebastiano Outside the Walls, the façade of Santa Susanna, Sant'Andrea al Quirinale, the portico of St. Peter's, San Carlo alle Quattro Fontane, the interior of the Basilica of San Giovanni in Lateran, the Church of Sant'Agnese in Piazza Navona, Santa Maria in Vallicella, San Giacomo agli Incurabili, Santa Luca and Martina, and many other churches, façades, and chapels designed by great architects who came to Rome from every part of Italy.

In the eighteenth century in Rome, a quieter Baroque style flowered with an orientation towards neoclassicism. Dating from this period are the façades of the Church of San Giovanni dei Fiorentini, San Giovanni in Lateran and Santa Maria Maggiore; also, the Church of Santa Maria della Morte, Sant'Apollinare, St. Celso and Giuliano in Banchi.

SANTA MARIA MAGGIORE

This basilica is dedicated to the worship of the Virgin. It is called Maggiore (meaning « largest » in Italian) because, among the many Roman churches dedicated to the Virgin, this is the largest. We owe its origin to a miraculous fact which happened in the time of Pope Liberius (352-66) on the night of August, 5, 352. The Pope and a pious Roman gentleman saw a vision of the Virgin from Whom they received the explicit recommendation of constructing a church on a point in Rome where, despite its being August, it would be snowing. The miracle of the snow in August was verified right on the Esquiline and in that place was erected the basilica, which was at first called Liberiana and named after Santa Maria of the Snow.

The grandiose **interior** of the Basilica is 86 meters long. It is divided into three naves, has a fine Cosmatesque paving, and a coffered ceiling in Renaissance style.

The early basilica was rebuilt by Sixtus III in 432-40; however, the original naves with the columns and the upper mosaics were conserved. ·In the twelfth century, Pope Eugenius III enlarged the atrium, while Nicholas IV rebuilt the apse. In 1670-76, Clement X reconstructed the rear façade and in 1740-58 Benedict XIV executed the principal façade. This church is the fourth patriarchal basilica after St. Peter's in the Vatican, San Giovanni in Lateran, and St. Paul Outside the Walls.

The interior of Santa Maria Maggiore. A view of the great mosaic by the Roman Jacopo Torriti (1295) which represents the « Redeemer seated enthroned with the Mother who receives the crown from His hands ». At the sides are a group of angels. On the left are the Apostles Peter and Paul with St. Francis. Kneeling is Pope Nicholas IV who commissioned the work. On the right are the Saints John the Baptist, Jacob and Anthony. Kneeling is the Cardinal Jacopo Colonna.

In the photo to the right, the baldacchino of the main altar by Ferdinando Fuga.

ST. PETER IN CHAINS

Eudossia, wife of the Emperor Valenti-
niano III, wished to have a basilica constructed to house the chains (in Latin « vincula »)
carried by St. Peter when he was imprisoned
in Jerusalem and Rome. From this came
the name of the church, St. Peter in Chains.
It was consecrated in 439 by Pope Sixtus III,
and restored in 774-95 by Adrian I. After
the year 1000 it underwent other restorations. During the Renaissance period Pope
Julius II made several modifications and in
the eighteenth century Francesco Fontana
added his work.

The Renaissance Façade with five arches
supported by octagonal pilasters, has been
attributed in the past to Baccio Pontelli,
but modern critics suggest the name Meo
di Caprino.

St. Peter in Chains. The spacious interior is divided into three naves by twenty very beautiful fluted marble columns with Doric capitals and Ionic bases. The wooden ceiling with curved vaults contains the fresco « *The Miracle of the Chains* » by G. B. Parodi. The circular tribune is frescoed by Giacomo Coppi (1577). The main altar with baldacchino is by Virginio Vespignani (1872). Below it is the urn which contains the chains of St. Peter.

St. Peter in Chains: « MOSES »

The greatness of Michelangelo Buonarroti may be seen in the right arm of the transept where we find the tomb of Pope Julius II della Rovere. The first great conception of the artist was renounced owing to causes beyond his control, however, his sculptoral genius may be appreciated in the statue of « Moses ». The great legislator of the Hebrew people, with a scornful and angry glance against the idolatrous Hebrews, is the synthesis of human and divine sentiments expressed in a pose full of dramatic tension, The masterpiece is also a reflection of the artist's state of mind, his character, and his most profound sentiments.

St. Peter in Chains: The chains of St. Peter. Here is the urn of gilded bronze (1856) which contains the precious reliquary, the chains which held the Apostle Peter during his imprisonment in Jerusalem and Rome.

THE BASILICA OF SAN GIOVANNI IN LATERAN

The basilica stands in the square bearing the same name. In the time of Nero, there were sumptuous houses belonging to the powerful Plauzi Laterani family in this square, thus, the name. When the family fell into disfavor, the Emperor confiscated their property which, passing from owner to owner, came into the dowry of Fausta, wife of the Emperor Constantine. He gave it to Pope Melchiade who on the property founded the basilica (311-14) and his own residence. Therefore, the first seat of the papacy was here, and the basilica was and still is the Cathedral of Rome.

The church of Pope Melchiade had five naves. It was so magnificent in its decorations, that it was called « golden » and named Salvatore. In the time of St. Gregory the Great it assumed the name of San Giovanni in honor of both the Baptist and the Evangelist. In the course of history, it had many unfortunate events. It was devastated by the Vandals, but then restored in the fifth century and again in the eighth century. It was damaged by the earthquake of 896 and rebuilt in 905. Nicholas IV decorated it splendidly in 1288-92, but a furious fire in 1308 destroyed it completely. It was then rebuilt by Clement V but underwent yet

The Holy Staircase is situated in Piazza San Giovanni in Lateran. The building was constructed by Domenico Fontana in the time of Sixtus V who wished to conserve the « Sancta Sanctorum », the antique private chapel of the Popes. The chapel was a part of the « Patriarchio », the old Papal residence which stood where the Palazzo Lateranense is now. Here, the Pope placed the stairway of honor of the residence which tradition identifies as the staircase ascended by Jesus in Pilate's palace in Jerusalem. The staircase was brought to Rome by St. Helena and consists of twenty-eight steps which the faithful climb on their knees.

San Giovanni in Lateran. A fine view of the façade, a masterpiece by the Florentine architect Alessandro Galilei. Imposing and monumental, it is composed of an architraved loggia and an arcaded open gallery. On Ascension Day, the Pope blesses the people from the central portico. On the roof are fifteen gigantic statues, seven meters high; in the center, Christ, at the sides the Saints John the Baptist and Evangelist with the Doctors of the Church. The façade was built in 1735. In the foreground is the antique **Door of St. John.**

another fire in 1361. Pope Urban V ordered the Siennese Giovanni di Stefano to completely rebuild it. The work was finished under the pontificate of Gregory XI. From then on, all the popes embellished the basilica, but in 1650 Pope Innocent X ordered a completely new building design from the architect Borromini. Of the antique part, he conserved only the apse which was then renewed in 1885 at the wish of Pope Leo XIII. It is important to remember that in this basilica Pope Boniface VIII proclaimed the first Holy Year in 1300.

The **interior** of San Giovanni in Lateran is 130 meters long and has five naves. Solemn and suggestive, it is animated by the colossal white statues of the Apostles placed in the niches of the pilasters. The wooden ceiling was probably designed by Pirro Ligorio. It was begun in 1562 and finished at the beginning of the nineteenth century with a competition of famous carvers.

The presbytery and the apse, as has been said, was not redesigned in 1885, however the mosaic of the apse is by Iacopo Torriti and Iacopo da Camerino (1288-94). They executed it for the original apse which we see here newly restored.

118

THE BASILICA OF ST. PAUL OUTSIDE THE WALLS

The basilica was built on the place where the Apostle St. Paul, martyred in 64-68, was buried. His tomb was conserved for worship by the faithful by a Christian matron called Lucina, who was the owner of the surrounding territory. In the time of Pope Anacletus in 103 an oratory was built which the Emperor Constantine wished to transform into a beautiful basilica in 324. In time, it became insufficient to contain the

A detail of the **Cloister** of **San Giovanni in Lateran.** Constructed by Vassalletto (1215-32), it is a true masterpiece of Cosmatesque art.

The Basilica of St. Paul Outside the Walls. The façade which overlooks the Tiber is preceded by a court designed by Guglielmo Calderini. The pronaos of the court is composed of ten monolithic columns. In the upper part, which is the work of Francesco Vespignani, we see mosaics executed from the designs of Filippo Agricola and Nicola Consoni. In front of the pronaos is the great statue of St. Paul sculpted by Giuseppe Obici.

throngs of faithful, so that in 385 it was demolished and a more spacious basilica was rebuilt.

Many are the misfortunes which befell this famous basilica since it was outside the walls and on an obligatory thoroughfare for entering the city. In 739 it underwent plundering by the Longobards, and in 847 by the Saracens, however it was respected by the Goths, the Vandals, and the Visigoths. To defend the basilica from attacks, Pope John VIII constructed a fortified citadel in 872. The famous basilica was enriched by works of art and restored at different times between 1500 and 1700. On the night of July 16 and 17 of 1823 it was destroyed by a fire. Its reconstruction began under Pope Leo XII and lasted almost a century under such architects as Pasquale Belli, Pietro Bosio, Pietro Camporese the Younger, and in particular Luigi Poletti.

We must remember that this is the largest basilica in Rome after St. Peter's. Its plan has the same dimensions as the Ulpia Basilica in the Trajan Forum.

The Cloister of St. Paul. The very beautiful cloister with small twin columns decorated in mosaic is also part of the Benedictine convent saved from the fire of 1823. Begun in the twelfth century, it was completed before 1214. It is mostly the work of Pietro Vassalletto.

The interior of the Basilica of St. Paul. It is divided into five naves and has eighty monolithic columns. It is 131.66 meters long, 65 meters wide, and 29.70 meters high. The principal nave which we see here in all its imposing spaciality is 24.60 meters wide. The architectural style is of a late neoclassic taste. Above the pediment runs a frieze with portraits in mosaic of 262 Popes beginning with St. Peter until John XXIII. The ceiling is coffered with a rich gilded decoration. In the middle is the coat-of-arms of Pope Pius IX who consecrated the basilica in 1854.

The Church of San Clemente. — · Dedicated to the third Pope after St. Peter, it is a typical and well-preserved example of a Roman mediaeval basilica. It was built in 1108 by Pasquale II. The interior is in a basilical form of three naves divided by sixteen Roman columns and a Cosmatesque floor. The frescoes by Masolino da Panicale are of particular importance and can be found in the Chapel of St. Catherine of Alexandria.

Santa Maria in Cosmedin. In Piazza Bocca della Verità, in front of the Temple of Vesta, this very ancient church built in the sixth century stands on the site of the Temple of Hercules. It was enlarged by Adrian I in the eighth century, transformed by Nicolas I, and restored many times, most recently by G. B. Giovenale in 1894-1899. He sacrificed the Baroque style façade of Giuseppe Sardi to return to the original mediaeval structure. The high bell-tower in Romanesque style dates from the twelfth century. To the left, the charming Baroque fountain by Carlo Francesco Bizzaccheri (1715) who collaborated with Francesco Moratti, sculptor of the two tritons supporting the shell.

This tasteful and imposing façade in an elegant Rococco style belongs to the **Basilica of Santa Croce in Jerusalem** and is by the architects Domenico Gregorini and Pietro Passalacqua (1743). The Basilica was founded by St. Helena, mother of the Emperor Constantine, to hold the precious reliquary of the wooden cross on which Jesus died.

A fine view of the façade and bell-tower of the **Church of San Giorgio in Velabro.** Perhaps built in the sixth century, it was reconstructed in the time of Leo II (682) and restored in 1926 by Antonio Muñoz who removed the Baroque decorations and instrusions from the interior. The façade and the bell-tower are in a perfect Romanesque style.

The façade of **Santa Maria in Trastevere** built in the twelfth century. In
the tympanum a mosaic by P. Cavallini. The portico has five arches and a
terrace above. On the balustrade are some seventeenth century statues by Carlo
Fontana added in 1702. The bell-tower is in Romanesque style.

A panoramic view of Rome. In the foreground are the **Churches of Santo Nome di Maria** and **Santa Maria di Loreto.**

ROMAN PANORAMAS AND WALKS

What can we say about panoramas and walks in Rome which has not already been said? In whatever part of the city one happens to be, there or right nearby, is a panorama and a walk. It may be limited to a view of characteristic streets. When one least expects it, one comes across new architectural lines, the swaying of folliage on the trees, winding vegetation which has no fear of dizzy heights, or ruins of the glorious past.

For those who wish to enjoy the picturesque views of Rome as it was, it is enough to visit the Esquiline, the Gianiculum, the Aventine, or the Celio. Here one finds oneself in front of a flowering of orchards and gardens where it is possible to escape the torments of the city traffic. For those who have the time, wandering from street to street, piazza to piazza, and to each antique and modern quarter brings great satisfaction. One discovers places full of old and new novelties. There is no danger of being bored by repetition. In fact it is this continuous transfiguration of the city which charms and subjugates us.

For the romantic, for those in love, or for those who are in search of feeling free, there are special panoramas and walks. Turning one's steps in the direction of the Gianiculum, the Palatine, or the Pincio will bring breathtaking views of the immense

This marvellous panorama enjoyed from the **Gianicolo,** places in evidence a fine nucleus of historical buildings.

The Gianicolo traces its name to the deity Giano whose cult was here. The monument to Garibaldi by the Florentine sculptor Emilio Gallori (1895) proudly watches over the city.

city at every hour of the day. The first light of sunrise, assailed by winds, the sun, or by rain; the evening gilded by a marvellous sunset; these pictorial aspects of the city are forever changing and they are unforgettable.

Piazza del Campo dei Fiori. An expanse of covered stalls makes this square the theatre of a picturesque and popular market. It almost makes us forget the fact that on this same site the main executions took place. In the background we see the rear of the statue of *Giordano Bruno* who was burnt here for heresy. His monument in bronze is by Ettore Ferrari (1887).

The Little Market of Porta Portese. In *Trastevere*, near the gate by the same name, this curious and unique market of old things and artistic objects is held on Sunday mornings. It is a true market place of small antiquaries.

From the splendid terrace of the **Pincio,** one may enjoy a magnificent view of Rome. Here, in ancient times were the gardens of Locullo and other Roman personalities. Among these were the Pinci after whom the hill is named. It was transformed into a park by Valadier (1809-14).

A view of the city taken from the **Pincio.** In the foreground the bell-tower and small dome of the Renaissance **Church of Santa Maria del Popolo.** In the distance, on the hill, the grandiose *Hotel Hilton.*

A panorama of **Piazza del Popolo** from the Pincio with the dome of St. Peter's in the distance.

The inscription on the fountain reads:

PAVLVS·QVINTVS·PONTIFEX·MAXIMVS
AQVAM·IN·AGRO·BRACCIANENSI
SALVBERRIMIS·E·FONTIBVS·COLLECTAM
VETERIBVS·AQVAE·ALSIETINAE·DVCTIBVS·RESTITVTIS
NOVISQVE·ADDITIS
XXXV·AB·MILLIARIO·DVXIT

ANNO·DOMINI·MDCXII·PONTIFICATVS·SVI·SEPTIMO

The Fontana Paola. Along the Gianicolo we see this splendid and monumental fountain erected by Pope Paul V to collect the ancient water which the Emperor Trajan brought to Rome from the Albani Hills. The work is by the architects Flaminio Ponzio and Giovanni Fontana (1612).

A suggestive and luminous night view of **Piazza della Repubblica** with the **Fountain of the Nymphs.**

The antique water clock of the Pincio is a charmng curiosity for tourists.

The Marble Stadium is by the Carrarese architect Enrico del Debbio. This elegant modern marble stadium is found in the Foro Italico. It holds twenty thousand spectators and is decorated around the top of the steps with sixty statues of atheletes. The podium at its base contains two groups of wrestlers, expressive and vigorous sculptures by the Perugian Aroldo Bellini.

139

The Catacombs of San Callisto. These are the most important catacombs in Rome. They were constructed in the second century and were the official cemetery of the first popes. An avenue of cypresses leads to the little church from which one descends into the catacombs. Here the crypt of the popes is visible as well as the crypt of Santa Cecilia with frescoes of the seventh and eighth centuries. One may also see the five cubicles of the Sacraments decorated with very important frescoes of the third century. Finally, there is the crypt of Pope Eusebius.

The Catacombs of San Sebastiano are composed of four levels of galleries. In the second one is the crypt of St. Sebastian. One may also see numerous early Christian inscriptions of allegorical animals, each one having some particular meaning.

THE CATACOMBS

The term catacombs comes from the Latin « catacumbas » which means « near the descent to the tombs ». Catacombs were adopted as burial places by the Christians between the first and the fourth centuries. Their entrance was always visible from the exterior until 250 A.D., the year of the persecution by the Emperor Decius. They were composed of long galleries which were sometimes as much as five storeys high, as in the case of the Catacombs of San Callisto, which are the most majestic in Rome.

Pigeonhole burying places were made inside the galleries where the bodies were placed. They were then closed up with marble slabs which had simple inscriptions on them.

The catacombs are not only important for the knowledge which they give us of the cult of early Christianity, but also for their primitive Christian art. This art is to be seen mainly in frescoes executed in a simplified but highly experimental technique. There are fine examples in the Catacombs of San Callisto and Santa Priscilla. Also, the artistic importance of the sarcophagi should not be overlooked. The one representing « The Good Shepherd » in the Lateran Museum, is a fine example of this art.

The Catacombs of Santa Domitilla are the most extensive in Rome. They date from the end of the first century and are the work of St. Domitilla, a relàtion of Emperor Domitian. The basilica, erected in the fourth century over the tombs of St. Nereo and Achilleo, is of particular interest, as is the Flavian hypogeum with decorations of the first century and the cubicle of Saint Petronilla.

The Museum of Roman Civilization. A detail of the great plastic model of Imperial Rome which is found in the Museum of Roman Civilization in the new district of EUR. In the sixty rooms of the museum there are numerous and interesting reconstructions of the buildings of Rome, from its origin up until its greatest splendour.

INDEX